YOU choose

Come Clean, Carlos

Tell the Truth

Sarah Eason

KU-328-870

It might be useful for parents or teachers to read our 'How to use this book' guide on pages 28–29 before looking at Carlos's dilemmas. The points for discussion on these pages are helpful to share with your child once you have read the book together.

First published in 2011 by Wayland

Copyright © Wayland 2011

Wayland
338 Euston Road
London NW1 3BH

Wayland Australia
Level 17/207 Kent Street
Sydney, NSW 2000

All rights reserved

Produced for Wayland by Calcium
Design: Paul Myerscough
Editor for Wayland: Camilla Lloyd
Illustrations by Ailie Busby

British Library Cataloguing in Publication Data

Eason, Sarah.
    Come clean, Carlos! Tell the truth.—(You choose!)
    1. Truthfulness and falsehood—Juvenile literature.
    2. Truthfulness and falsehood—Juvenile fiction.
    I. Title II. Series
    177.3–dc22

ISBN: 978 0 7502 6644 4

Printed in China

Wayland is a division of Hachette Children's Books,
an Hachette UK company.
www.hachette.co.uk

CAVAN COUNTY LIBRARY
ACC No. C/260097
CLASS NO. 30–4
INVOICE NO 9108
PRICE 10.26

Cavan County Library
Withdrawn Stock

Class No. Jo·4   Acc No. C/260097

Author: Eason, S   Loc: – 7 JUN 2012

LEABHARLANN   – 5 JAN 2012
CHONDAE AN CHABHAIN

1. **This book may be kept three weeks. It is to be returned on / before the last date stamped below.**
2. A fine of 25c will be charged for every week or part of w
(Code 23)

MAR 2012		
2 4 AUG 2012		
		1 2 DEC 2012
0 3 APR 2013		

Contents

Hello, Carlos! 4

Fix it, Carlos 6

Be kind, Carlos 10

Don't worry, Carlos 14

Be careful, Carlos 18

Be true, Carlos 22

Well done, Carlos! 26

How to use this book 28

Glossary 30

Index 31

Hello, Carlos!

Carlos is **confused**. He knows he is supposed to come clean and tell the truth, but he doesn't always understand why. Sometimes, telling **fibs** seems much easier, and it stops him being told off for things he has done.

CAVAN COUNTY LIBRARY

Follow Carlos as he finds himself in tricky situations in which he must choose to be **honest**.

YOU choose too!

Fix it, Carlos

Carlos is playing football in the garden.

WHOOPS! His shot goes wide and smashes a flowerpot to pieces.

What should Carlos choose to do?

Should Carlos:

a tell Dad he's
really sorry,
and he'll be more
careful next time?

b hide all the
flowerpot pieces
behind the
garden shed?

8

c dig a plant up from the garden to fill the space?

Carlos, choose **a**

Of course it's bad to break things, but **accidents** happen and it's worse to lie about them. Most grown-ups get more cross about lies than accidents. It's best to be brave and come clean.

What would **YOU** choose to do?

Be kind, Carlos

Carlos's friend, James, is being really **mean** to another boy, Owen, at school.

Carlos's teacher wants to know what's going on.

What should Carlos choose to do?

Should Carlos:

a say it was some big girls who picked on Owen?

b tell the truth – James was being mean to Owen?

c pretend he doesn't know anything about it?

Carlos, choose **b**

It's really important to tell the truth if somebody is being picked on. Who wants a friend who is mean? If you tell the truth, the unkindness might stop and everyone can be friends.

What would YOU choose to do?

Don't worry, Carlos

Two of Carlos's friends are going to Disneyland for their holiday.

Carlos **wishes** he was going to Disneyland too.

What should Carlos choose to do?

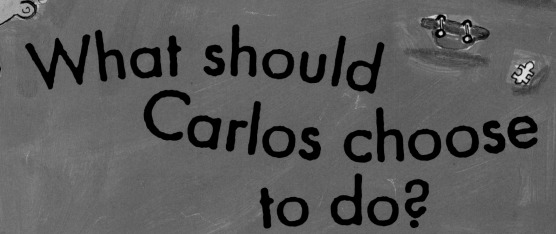

Should Carlos:

a tell his Dad that he must take him to Disneyland for a **school project?**

b tell his friends he's been to Disneyland and it was very boring?

C get excited about his own holiday at the seaside, doing fun things with his Dad?

Carlos, choose **C**

You don't have to do the same things as your friends to have fun. And you certainly don't need to make things up to keep them as your friends! Good friends will like you if you are honest and don't fib.

What would YOU choose to do?

Be careful, Carlos

Carlos wants to ride his scooter around the block on his own, like some of his friends do.

His Dad says Carlos must wait until he is older. He is not big enough to ride on his own just yet.

What should Carlos choose to do?

Should Carlos:

a ask his Dad to go with him to **prove** that he is very careful?

b scoot off, even though his Dad shouts 'Stop!'?

c say that all his friends are allowed to go on their own, even if they are not?

Carlos, choose **a**

Don't make things up to get your own way! And don't go against someone's wishes, either. Grown-ups just want to keep you safe. Show that you can be trusted and you will be allowed to do more.

What would **YOU** choose to do?

Be true, Carlos

Carlos is really **bored**.

He starts to **doodle** on the walls of his bedroom and makes a mark. Yikes – what a mess!

What should Carlos choose to do?

Should Carlos:

a move a poster to cover up his wall art?

b tell his Dad that the tooth fairy drew on the wall?

C say sorry and help to clean off the mark?

Carlos, choose **C**

Saying sorry is always better than telling a fib. Grown-ups want to know that they can trust you. Try to think of good ways to make up for your **mistakes**, instead of **lying** about them.

What would **YOU** choose to do?

Well done, Carlos!

Hey, look at Carlos! Now he knows how to make truthful choices, he's feeling much **happier**.

Did you choose the right thing to do each time? If you did, big cheers for you!

If you chose some of the other answers, try to think about Carlos's choices to help you make truthful choices next time. Then it will be big smiles all round!

It's always good to come clean!

How to use this book

This book can be used by a grown-up and a child together. It is based on common situations that might tempt any child to tell a lie. Invite your child to talk about each of the choices. Ask questions such as 'Why do you think Carlos should tell his Dad that he's drawn on his wall?'.

Discuss the wrong choices, as well as the right ones, with your child. Describe what is happening in the following pictures and talk about what the wrong and right choices might be.

• Listen to grown-ups – they have reasons for saying 'No', even if they don't always explain them.

• Covering up for mean people makes things worse. They can then carry on being mean to even more people.

- Don't make up stories to avoid telling the truth – you just make an even bigger fib!

- Don't cover up an accident. It's better to tell the truth.

Ask your child to think about why people tell fibs. Does it make things easier? Point out what happens when the truth comes out – usually, the fibber ends up in even bigger trouble! If a child constantly tells lies, people find it hard to believe them even when they are telling the truth.

Help your child to realise through explaining and role play that grown-ups need to trust them – then they are more likely to allow children to do the things they want to do. In return, try to make sure your child feels they can own up to you if they need to!

CAVAN COUNTY LIBRARY

Glossary

accidents   when something goes wrong by mistake, such as breaking a flowerpot or a window

confused   to not understand something

doodle   to draw

fibs   lies

lying   not telling the truth

mean   to be unkind

mistakes   doing something wrong or getting something wrong

prove   to show someone that something is true

school project   a special piece of work done at school or for your homework

wishes   hoping for something

Index

accidents 9

being brave 9
being kind 10–13

choosing the right thing
26–27

feeling bored 22–25
friends 10, 13, 14, 16, 17,
18, 21

hiding things 8, 24

mistakes 8, 25

playing 6, 18

telling lies 4, 9, 12, 13,
16, 17, 21, 24, 25
telling the truth 4, 5,
8, 9, 12, 13, 17, 25,
26, 27
trust 21, 25

Titles in the series

ISBN: 978 0 7502 6644 4

Like all children, Carlos sometimes does things that are wrong, and doesn't come clean. He has lots of choices to make – but which are the TRUTHFUL ones?

ISBN: 978 0 7502 6642 0

Like all children, Charlie sometimes feels a little scared. He has lots of choices to make – but which are the BRAVE ones?

ISBN: 978 0 7502 6645 1

Like all children, Gertie sometimes plays a little dirty. We put Gertie on the spot with some tricky problems and ask her to decide what is FAIR!

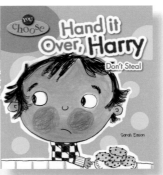

ISBN: 978 0 7502 6643 7

Like all children, Harry sometimes takes things that don't belong to him. He has lots of choices to make – but which are the HONEST ones?